Elena Kats-Chernin

For Alex
for violin and piano

T0078749

2004

Violin part edited by
Robyn Sarajinsky

Score and part

BOOSEY & HAWKES
BOTE & BOCK

Elena Kats-Chernin
For Alex
for violin and piano
(2004)

Violin part edited by Robyn Sarajinsky

Duration: 5′

www.boosey.com

BB 3594

ISMN 979-0-2025-3594-3
ISBN 978-3-7931-4291-1

Copyright © 2004 by Boosey & Hawkes, Inc.
Copyright © 2010 assigned to Boosey & Hawkes · Bote & Bock, Berlin.
Copyright for all countries. All rights reserved.

For Alex
for violin and piano

No. 1 (Robyn's Request)

ELENA KATS-CHERNIN
Violin part edited by Robyn Sarajinsky

31st January, 2004

Copyright © 2004 by Boosey & Hawkes, Inc.
Copyright © 2010 assigned to Boosey & Hawkes · Bote & Bock, Berlin.
Copyright for all countries. All rights reserved.

20210526

No. 2 (Robyn's Request)

31st, January, 2004

No. 2a (Robyn's Request)

20210526

Violin

For Alex
for violin and piano

No. 1 (Robyn's Request)

ELENA KATS-CHERNIN
Violin part edited by Robyn Sarajinsky

No. 2 (Robyn's Request)

Copyright © 2004 by Boosey & Hawkes, Inc.
Copyright © 2010 assigned to Boosey & Hawkes · Bote & Bock, Berlin.
Copyright for all countries. All rights reserved.

20210526

No. 2a (Robyn's Request)

A more advanced version of piece No. 2

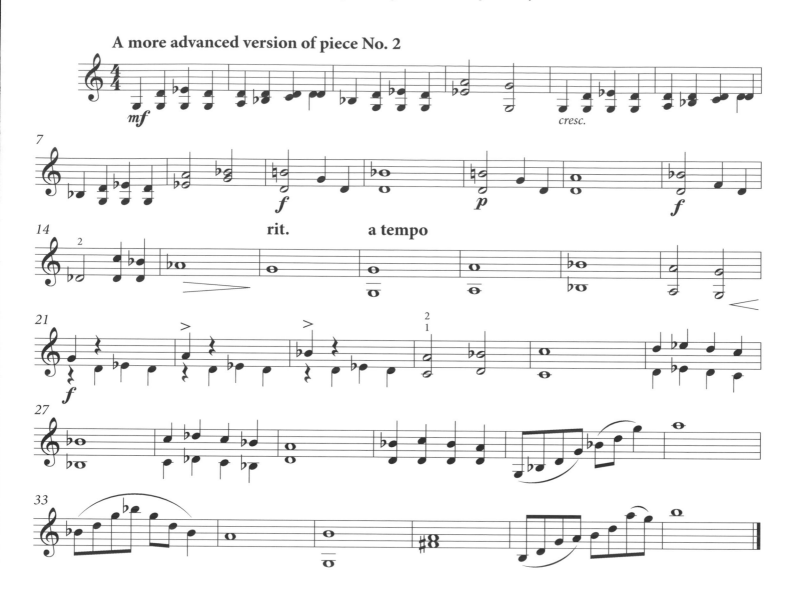

No. 3 (Robyn's Request)

"Almost a folk song"

It is optional to repeat the whole piece, 2nd time Violin plays pizz.

20210526

No. 4 (Robyn's Request)

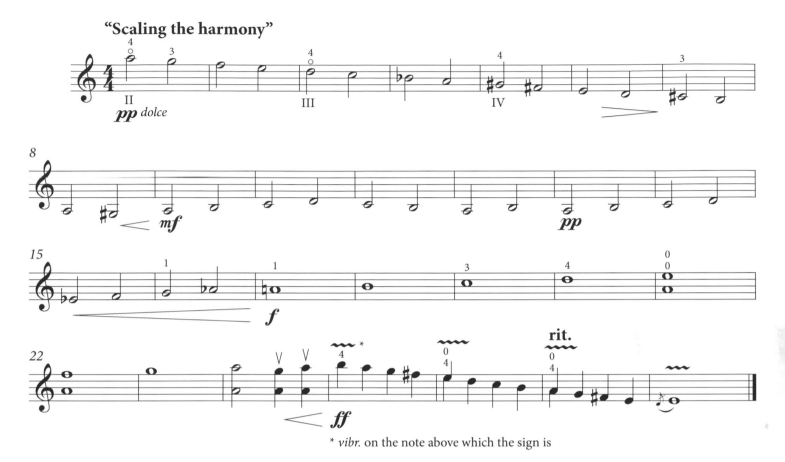

*vibr. on the note above which the sign is

No. 5 (Robyn's Request)

Violin

No. 6 (Robyn's Request)

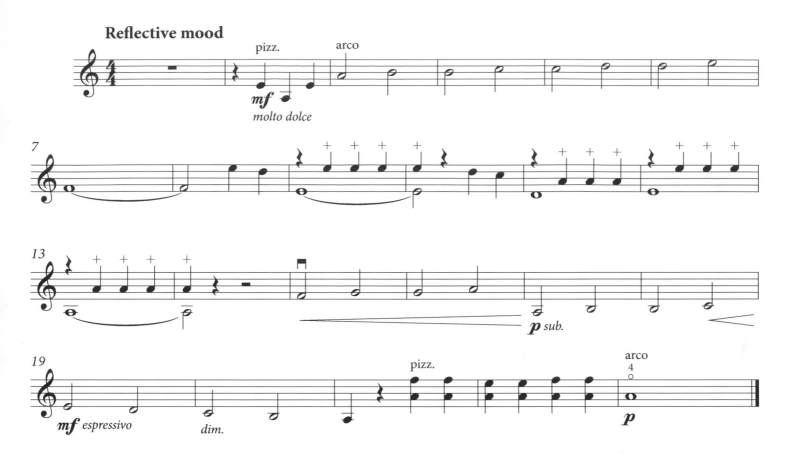

ISMN 979-0-2025-3594-3   ISBN 978-3-7931-4291-1

BOOSEY & HAWKES
Bote & Bock

20210526

31st, January, 2004

No. 3 (Robyn's Request)

"Almost a folk song"

It is optional to repeat the whole piece, 2nd time Violin plays pizz.

1st February, 2004
Coogee
20210526

No. 4 (Robyn's Request)

* *vibr.* on the note above which the sign is

1st February 2004
Coogee

20210526

No. 5 (Robyn's Request)

No. 6 (Robyn's Request)

1st February, 2004
Coogee
20210526